# R. VAUGHAN WILLIAMS

# NORFOLK RHAPSODY NO. 2

EDITED AND COMPLETED BY
## STEPHEN HOGGER

STUDY SCORE

MUSIC DEPARTMENT

## OXFORD
UNIVERSITY PRESS

# OXFORD
UNIVERSITY PRESS

Great Clarendon Street, Oxford OX2 6DP,
United Kingdom

Oxford University Press is a department of the University of Oxford.
It furthers the University's objective of excellence in research, scholarship,
and education by publishing worldwide. Oxford is a registered trade mark of
Oxford University Press in the UK and in certain other countries

First published 2014

Impression: 2

ISBN 978-0-19-340341-3 (study score)
ISBN 978-0-19-339975-4 (on hire)

Music origination by Andrew Jones

Printed in Great Britain
by Caligraving Ltd, Thetford, Norfolk

# PREFACE

Ralph Vaughan Williams originally planned that his three Norfolk Rhapsodies should form a Norfolk Symphony, with the second rhapsody constituting a telescoped slow movement and a Scherzo. *Norfolk Rhapsody No. 1* has long been in the repertoire but Nos. 2 and 3 have not been played since 1914, and unfortunately No. 3 has not survived. All three were composed in 1906 and the first was performed in August of that year at The Queen's Hall in London by the Queen's Hall Orchestra, conducted by Henry Wood. The other two were premiered on 27 September 1907 at Park Hall in Cardiff by the London Symphony Orchestra, conducted by the composer.

*Norfolk Rhapsody No. 2* opens with a three-bar introduction played by a solo cello before the woodwind take up the first tune, 'Young Henry the Poacher', the last two phrases being repeated by the strings as a refrain. It is then heard in varied form in the violas and cellos. The tempo becomes more animated until the climax is reached, when the second theme, 'All on Spurn Point', is hinted at firstly by the strings, then the horns, followed by the oboe. This melody then appears in its complete form as a horn solo before being repeated by a combination of instruments; after an extended cadence the third tune, 'The Saucy Bold Robber', forms the basis of the scherzo section. An accompanying figure is set up by the strings using material derived from the last bar of the tune, which itself is heard on the piccolo and oboe, followed by the full woodwind section. After a brief attempt at a canon, the scherzo dies away and the first theme returns accompanied by tremolando violas. The work ends with a pianissimo reference to 'Spurn Point'. All three songs used in *Norfolk Rhapsody No. 2* had been collected by Vaughan Williams in King's Lynn on 9 and 10 January 1905.

There are two pages missing from the original manuscript held in the British Library, which probably consisted of around nine or ten bars of music, forming the extended cadence mentioned above (bars 85–93 in the present edition). I was approached by Richard Hickox, with the agreement of Michael Kennedy from RVW Ltd, to complete and edit *Norfolk Rhapsody No. 2* following the tremendous success of Chandos's recording of the original version of *A London Symphony*, which I had edited in 2000.

A fragment of manuscript paper tucked in the back of the original manuscript contained three bars in Vaughan Williams's hand, which I was able to include in the missing section as they consisted of material from bars 82–4; these now form bars 87–90. The presence of these jottings may indicate that Vaughan Williams was aware that the two pages had gone missing and had begun to remedy the situation. I have preceded these bars by two quoting the horn solo from the beginning of 'Spurn Point', and followed them with four bars that form a modulatory bridge from E flat major to B minor (bar 90) and the beginning of the scherzo (bars 91–3), with the accompaniment and orchestration derived from bars 94–109.

A recording of this edition, together with *Norfolk Rhapsody No. 1*, *The Running Set*, and Symphony No. 3, performed by the London Symphony Orchestra and conducted by Richard Hickox, is available on the Chandos label (CHAN 10001).

Stephen Hogger
July 2014

# ORCHESTRATION

2 FLUTES (1st doubling Piccolo)

2 OBOES

COR ANGLAIS

2 CLARINETS (in B♭)

2 BASSOONS

4 HORNS (in F)

2 TRUMPETS (in F)*

2 TROMBONES

BASS TROMBONE

TUBA

TIMPANI

PERCUSSION (Triangle)

HARP

STRINGS

* Parts for Trumpets in B♭ are also available on hire/rental

Duration: *c.*9 minutes

# Norfolk Rhapsody No. 2 in D minor

RALPH VAUGHAN WILLIAMS
Edited and completed by Stephen Hogger

Printed in Great Britain

OXFORD UNIVERSITY PRESS, MUSIC DEPARTMENT, GREAT CLARENDON STREET, OXFORD OX2 6DP

4

**meno mosso**

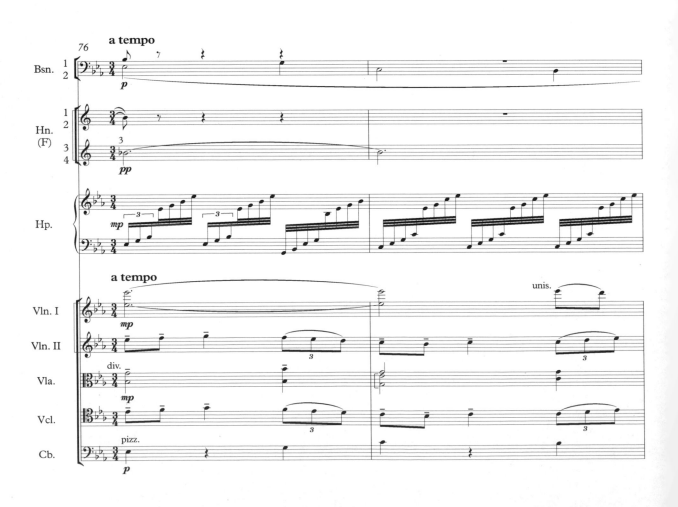

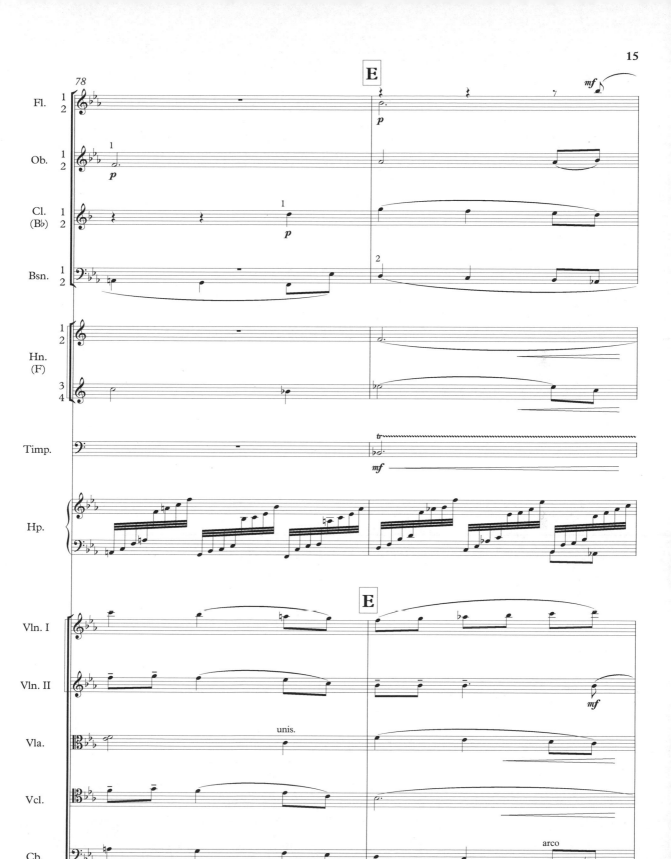